You mig be from Saskatchewan

D0462043

if...

volume 2

CARSON DEMMANS
JASON SYLVESTRE

MacIntyre Purcell Publishing Inc.
194 Hospital Rd.
Lunenburg, Nova Scotia
B0J 2C0
902-640-2337
www.macintyrepurcell.com
info@macintyrepurcell.com

Printed and bound in Canada by Marquis.

Library and Archives Canada Cataloguing in Publication

Demmans, Carson, author   You might be from Saskatchewan if...Volume 2 / [written by] Carson Demmans ; [illustrated by] Jason Sylvestre.

ISBN 978-1-927097-48-9 (pbk.)

1. Saskatchewan--Social life and customs--Caricatures and cartoons. 2. Canadian wit and humor, Pictorial (English).   I. Sylvestre, Jason, illustrator II. Title.

FC3511.3.D443 2014   971.24   C2014-902510-6

MacIntyre Purcell Publishing Inc. would like to acknowledge the financial support of the Government of Canada through Department of Canadian Heritage (Canada Book Fund) and the Nova Scotia Department of Tourism, Culture and Heritage.

Canadian Patrimoine
Heritage canadien

FOREWORD

After spending all of my early years in Saskatchewan, I moved to California to coach the San Jose Sharks. During my time in Melville, Goodsoil, and Saskatoon, I thought I had heard every Saskatchewan joke possible. Then one day a mysterious package arrived from the author of this book, who I happened to have gone to high school with (Okay, so the old joke about Saskatchewan being so small that everyone knows everyone else is true; it's funny, but it's still true).

The package contained the first volume in this series. I read it. I laughed. What guy from Saskatchewan wouldn't laugh at jokes about perogies, bad roads, bad weather, and hockey, even if he does live in California now?

Then I was given an advance copy of the second volume in the series. I read it and laughed, proving there is no limit to the amount of jokes you can make about perogies, bad roads, bad weather, hockey, and a hundred other things that define Saskatchewan.

When Carson asked me to help him out by writing this foreword, we hadn't communicated with each other for more than 20 years. Naturally, I said yes.

That's what people from Saskatchewan do, right?

Now, let this book help you out by making you laugh.

— **Todd McLellan**
Coach, San Jose Sharks

"The human race has one really effective weapon, and that is laughter."

— Mark Twain

This book is dedicated to my loving wife Shelley, who proves she has a great sense of humour everytime she sticks with me for one more day.

— Carson Demmans

To my family and friends, who make every day fun.

— Jason Sylvestre

The Journey Begins . . .

WHEN OTHER PEOPLE SEE A GANGSTA IN A HOODIE,
ALL YOU SEE IS A HOSER IN A BUNNYHUG.

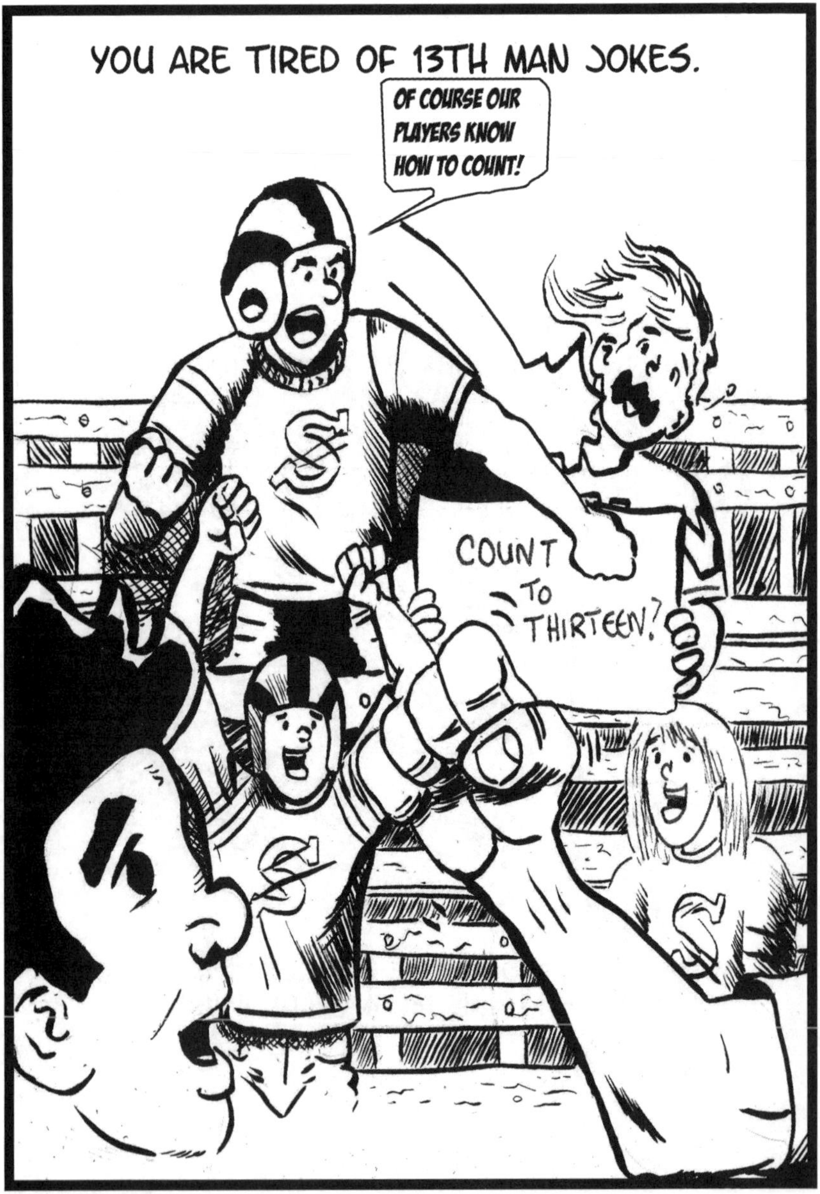
YOU ARE TIRED OF 13TH MAN JOKES.
OF COURSE OUR PLAYERS KNOW HOW TO COUNT!
COUNT TO THIRTEEN?

DURING WINTER, HALF OF YOUR FAMILY IS IN ARIZONA.

YOU HAVE TO SHOVEL **BEFORE** YOU USE YOUR SNOW BLOWER.

YOU LIVE IN TOWN, BUT YOUR NEIGHBOUR DOESN'T.

YOU HAVE NEVER BEEN TO A BIG CITY,
BUT YOU KNOW WHAT A TRAFFIC JAM IS.

YOU HAVE NEVER UNDERSTOOD THE BANJO BOWL JOKE, BECAUSE YOU KNOW HILLBILLIES, AND THEY DON'T PLAY BANJOES (BUT YOU WISH THEY DID).

YOU AND YOUR FRIENDS HAVE RE-ENACTED
THE MUSICAL RIDE.

IT DOESN'T MATTER IF "CORNER GAS" AND "LITTLE MOSQUE ON THE PRAIRIE" WENT OFF AIR, BECAUSE YOU LIVE THEM.

YOU HAVE SEEN THE WIND, AND IT'S NOT A PRETTY SIGHT!

YOU HAVE LOST YOUR CAR IN A PARKING LOT, BUT NOT JUST BECAUSE YOU FORGOT WHERE YOU PARKED IT!

YOU GO TO CHURCH REGULARLY, BUT NOT FOR THE SERVICE.

YOU HAVE BEEN TO DEMOLITION DERBYS
THAT DIDN'T INVOLVE CARS.

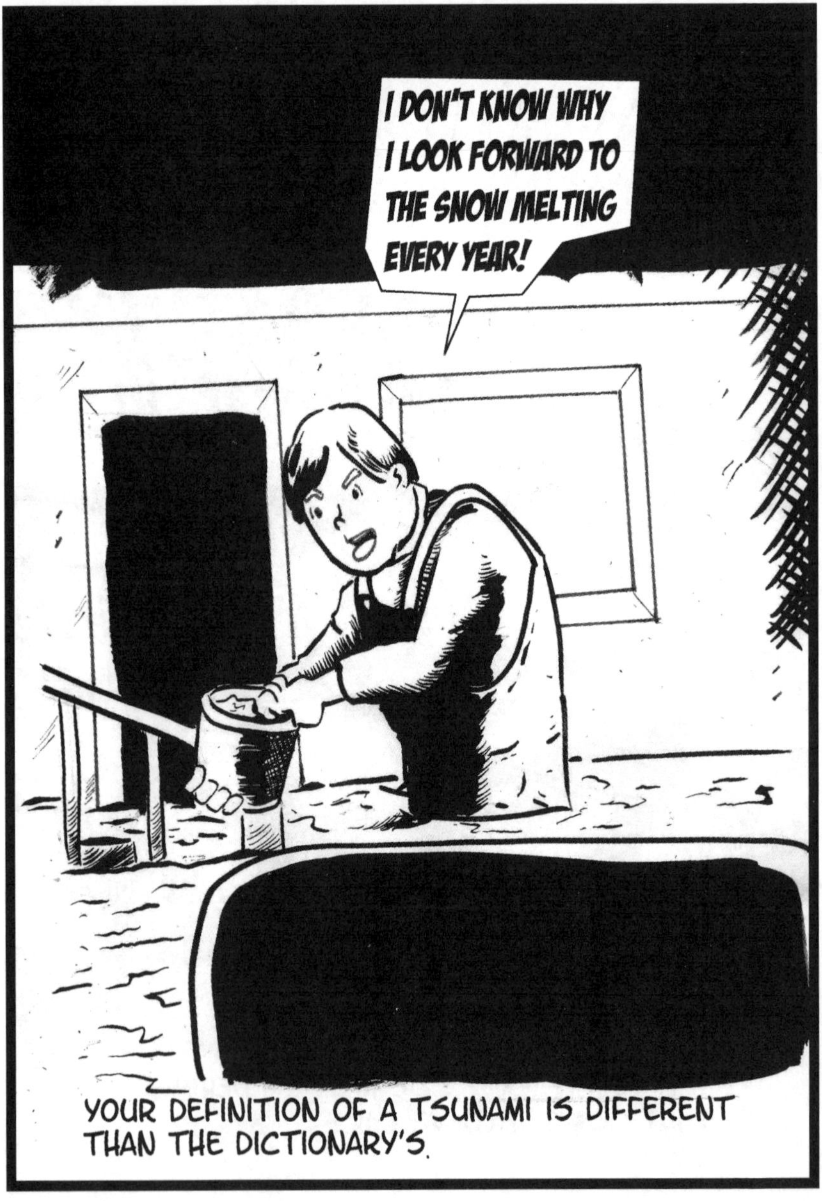
I DON'T KNOW WHY I LOOK FORWARD TO THE SNOW MELTING EVERY YEAR!
YOUR DEFINITION OF A TSUNAMI IS DIFFERENT THAN THE DICTIONARY'S.

AFTER ANOTHER WINTER OF MINUS 30 TEMPERA-
TURES, YOU SERIOUSLY CONSIDER HIBERNATION.

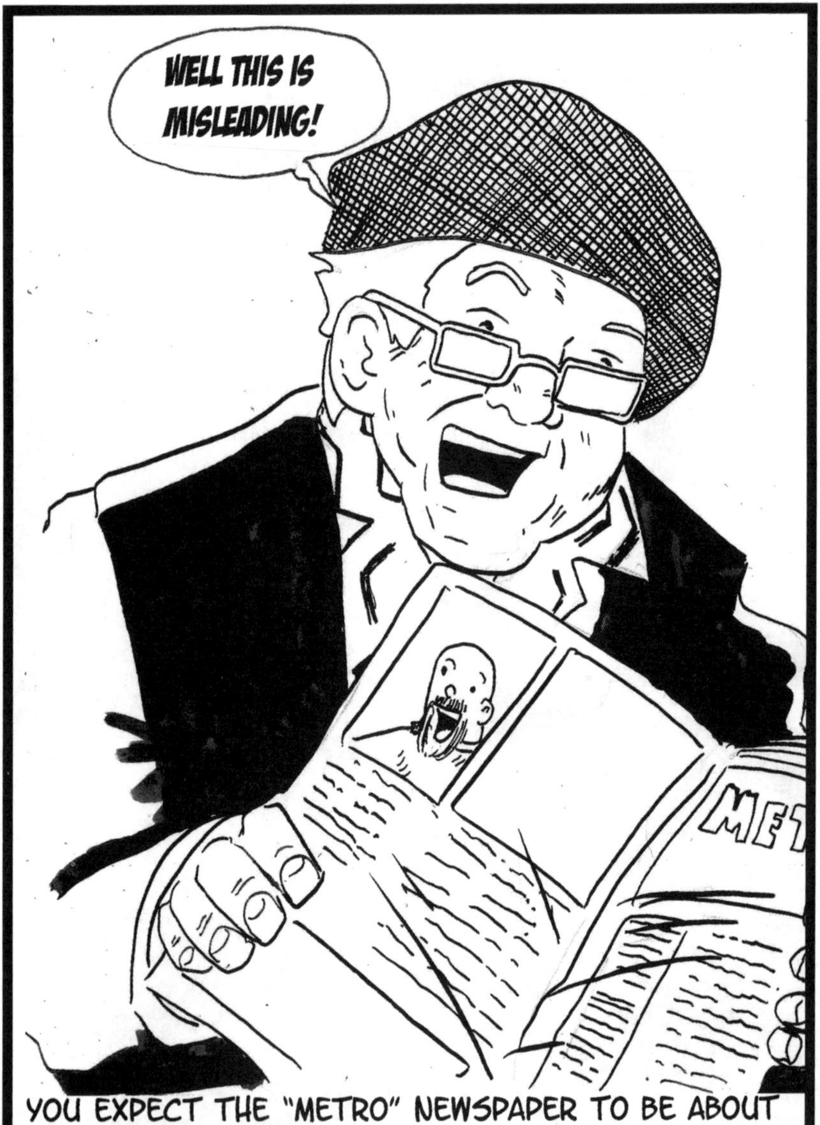
WELL THIS IS MISLEADING!
METR
YOU EXPECT THE "METRO" NEWSPAPER TO BE ABOUT "METRO THE COMEDIAN".

YOU HAVE LOOKED TO SEE IF DICK ASSMAN HAS A STAR ON THE CANADIAN WALK OF FAME.

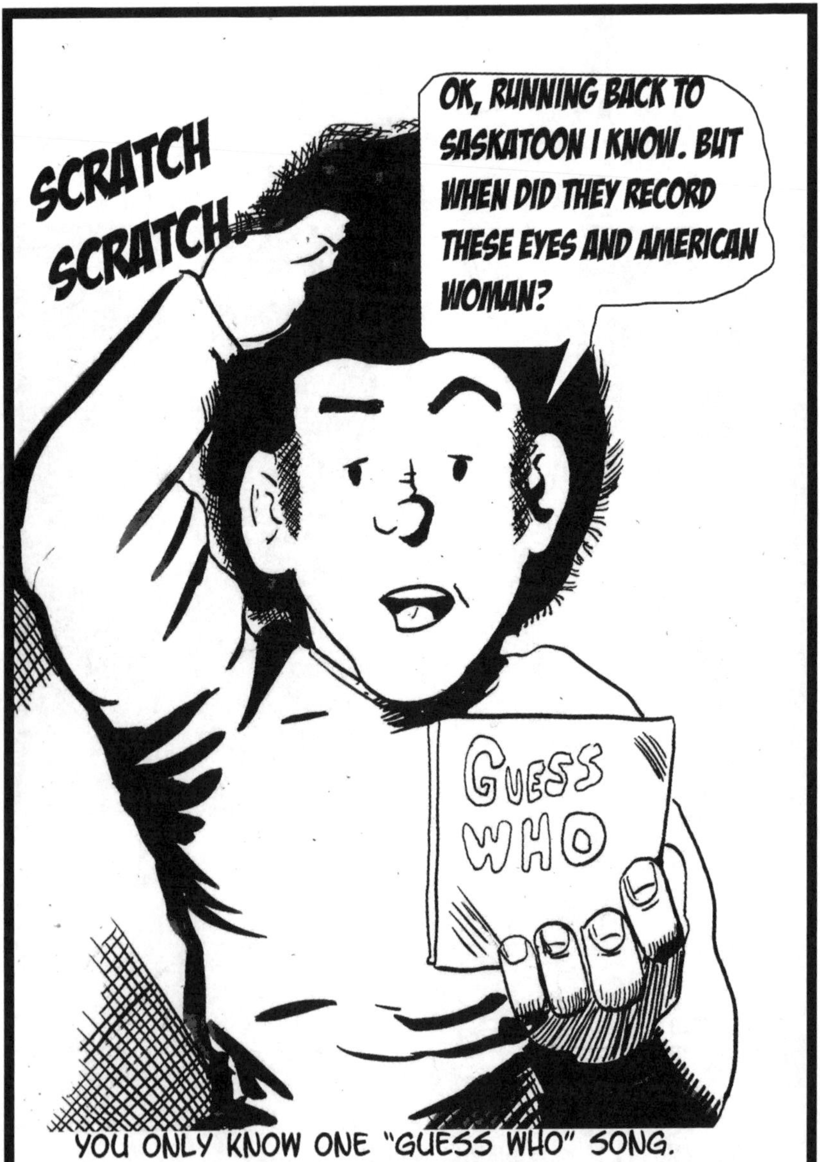
SCRATCH SCRATCH...
OK, RUNNING BACK TO SASKATOON I KNOW. BUT WHEN DID THEY RECORD THESE EYES AND AMERICAN WOMAN?
GUESS WHO
YOU ONLY KNOW ONE "GUESS WHO" SONG.

YOUR FAMILY CAMPS IN THE BACK YARD, AND THEY STILL SEE WILDLIFE.

YOU SCORED A HOLE IN ONE, BUT IT WAS THE WRONG HOLE!

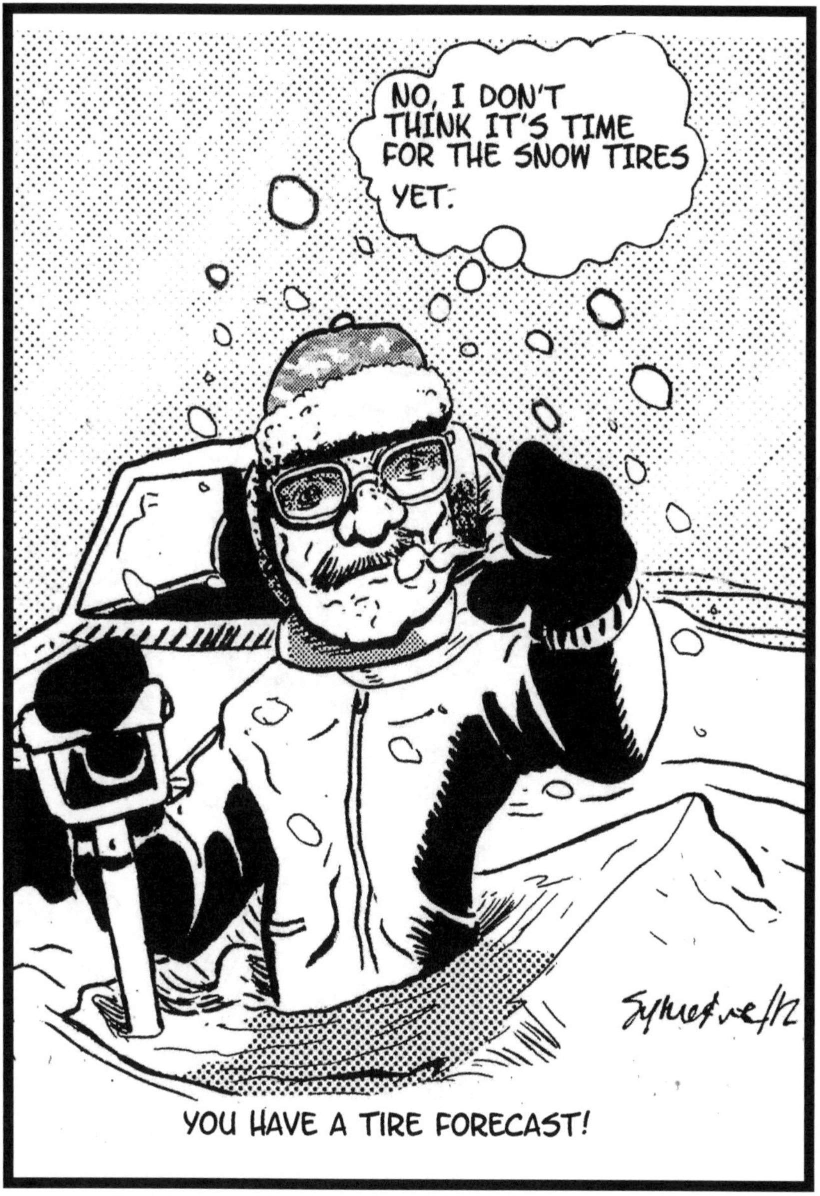
NO, I DON'T THINK IT'S TIME FOR THE SNOW TIRES YET.
YOU HAVE A TIRE FORECAST!

THE FIRST PART OF YOUR CAR TO WEAR OUT IS YOUR SUSPENSION.

YOUR BACKYARD HAS DOUBLED AS A SECOND FREEZER.

YOU TAKE AN ELEVATOR DOWN TO WORK, NOT UP.

THE JOKE OF GIVING PEOPLE FROM OUT OF PROVINCE A "PRAIRIE OYSTER" AND THEN TELLING THEM WHAT IT IS AFTER THEY EAT IT, NEVER GETS OLD.

IT TAKES MORE THAN LOCKING YOUR COOLER IN A CAR
TO KEEP BEARS AWAY FROM IT WHEN YOU GO CAMPING.

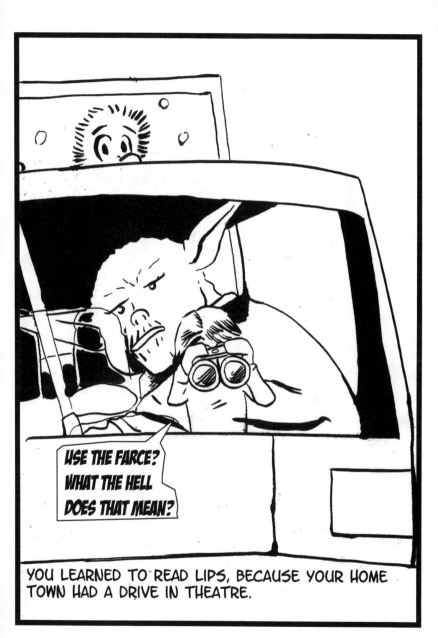

YOU LEARNED TO READ LIPS, BECAUSE YOUR HOME TOWN HAD A DRIVE IN THEATRE.

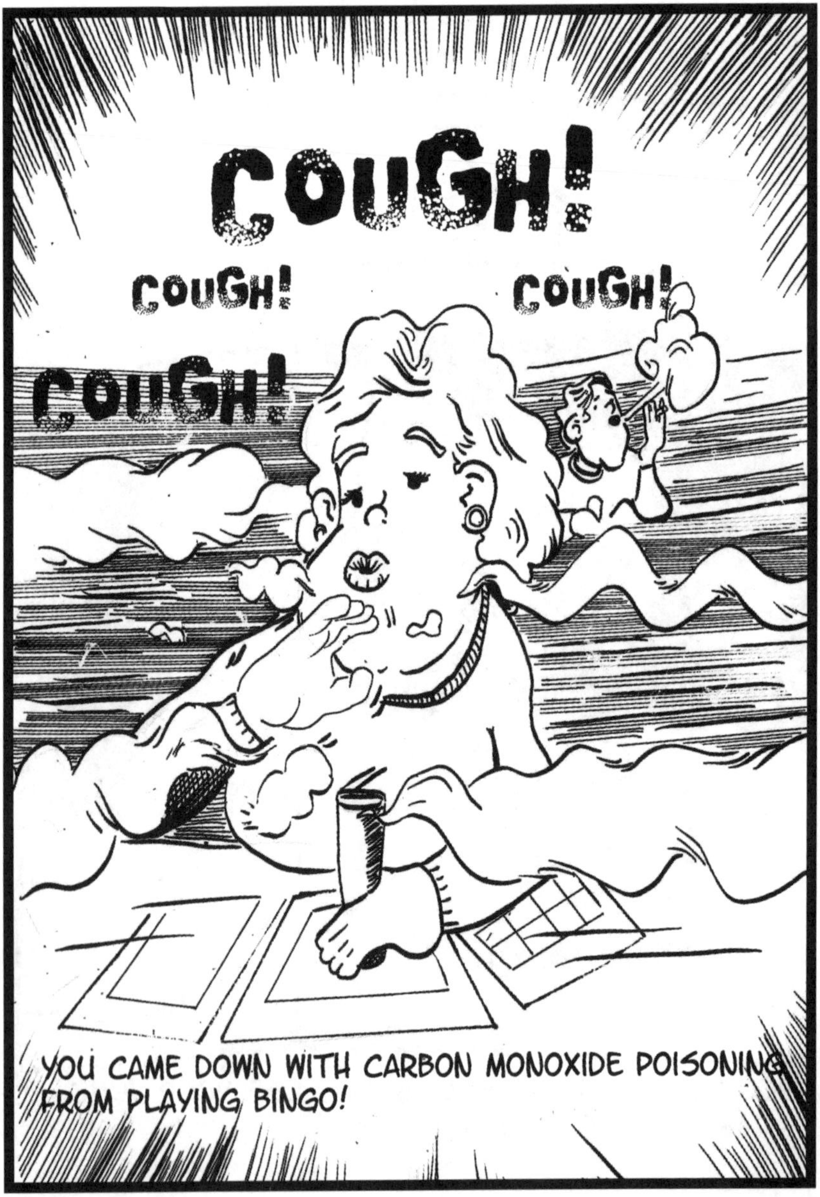
COUGH!
COUGH!
COUGH!
COUGH!
YOU CAME DOWN WITH CARBON MONOXIDE POISONING FROM PLAYING BINGO!

YOU TURN GREEN WITH PRIDE, NOT ENVY.

YOU HAVE WORN AN ORGANIC HAT TO A FOOTBALL GAME.

YOUR NEIGHBOUR GOT A DELUXE RAIN GAUGE,
SO YOU GOT A SUPER DELUXE RAIN GAUGE.

YOU HAVE BOUGHT A SLURPEE IN THE MIDDLE OF THE WINTER.

YOU HAVE CRIED DURING A WEATHER FORECAST.

YOU HAVE FOUND SNOW UNDER YOUR SHRUBS IN JUNE THAT STILL HASN'T MELTED.

YOU HAVE HAD SO MANY TICKS, THAT THE COAT OF ARMS FOR YOUR PROVINCE STARTS TO LOOK LIKE ONE.

41

HERE'S ANOTHER ONE!

YOU AND YOUR SPOUSE GET TWO INVITATIONS TO THE SAME FAMILY REUNION, BECAUSE YOUR SPOUSE'S COUSIN'S COUSIN IS YOU.

Your hockey rink has potholes.

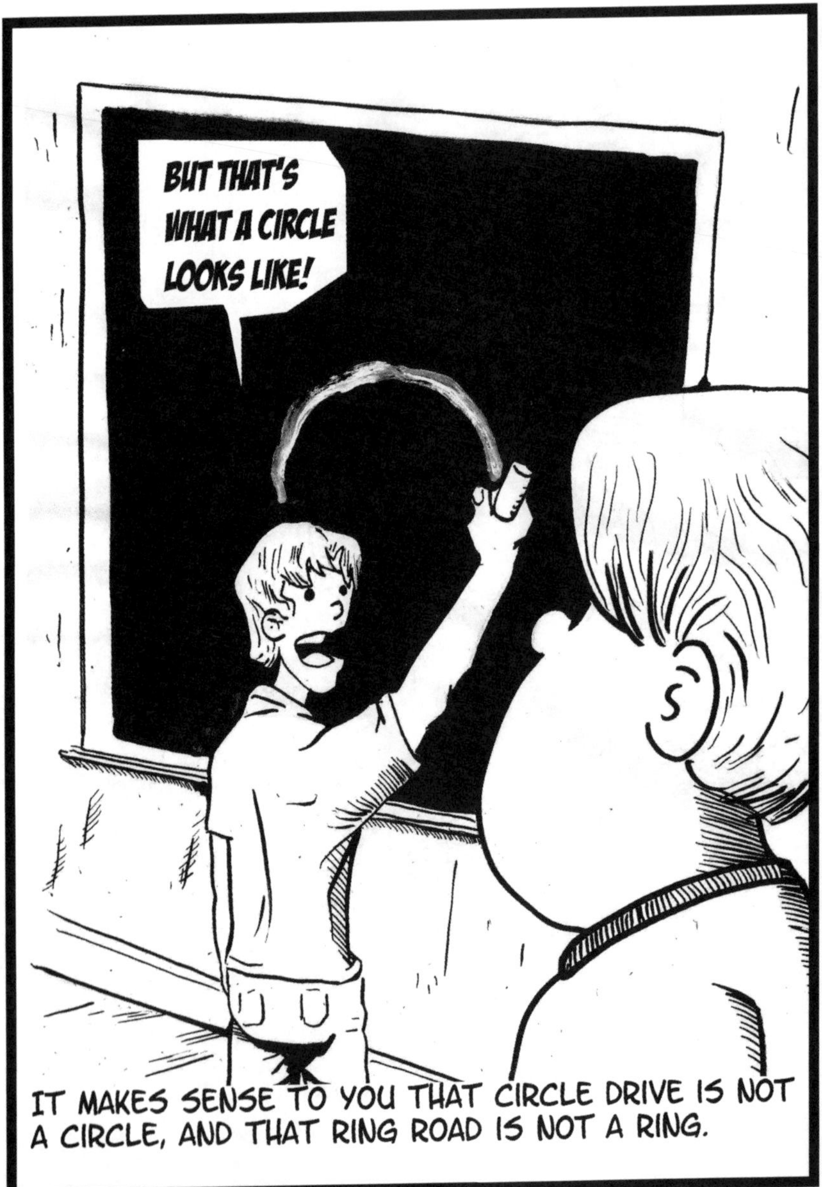
BUT THAT'S WHAT A CIRCLE LOOKS LIKE!
IT MAKES SENSE TO YOU THAT CIRCLE DRIVE IS NOT A CIRCLE, AND THAT RING ROAD IS NOT A RING.

YOUR CITY HAD NO SCENERY, SO THEY MADE SOME.

THE MOST FAMOUS PERSON TO COME FROM YOUR TOWN IS A GOPHER.

YOUR TREES ARE WHITE IN THE WINTER FROM THE SNOW, AND IN THE SUMMER FROM THE CATERPILLARS.

YOU HAVE HAD PEOPLE OVER TO SEE A CARROT.

YOUR HOME GYM HAS ALL NATURAL INGREDIENTS.

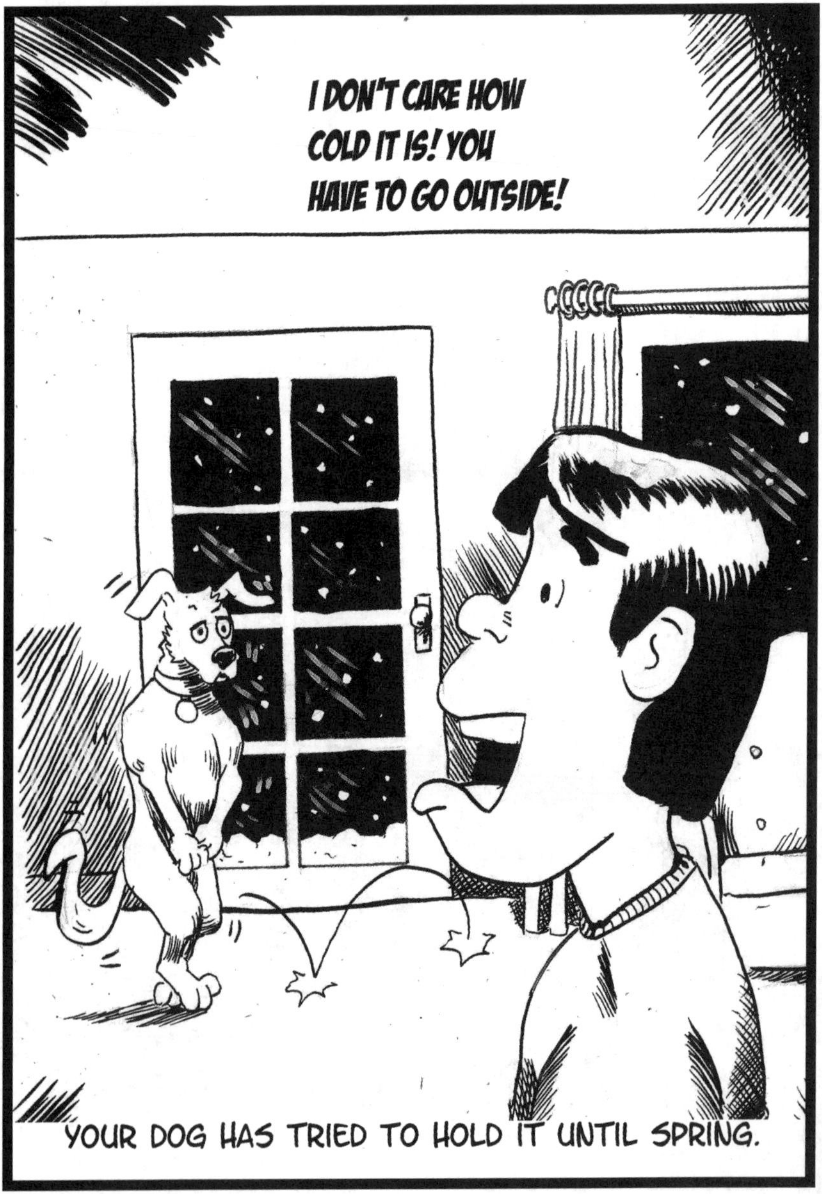
I DON'T CARE HOW COLD IT IS! YOU HAVE TO GO OUTSIDE!
YOUR DOG HAS TRIED TO HOLD IT UNTIL SPRING.

YOU BOUGHT "50 SHADES OF GREY" ASSUMING IT WAS A BOOK OF BEAUTY TIPS.

HOW HARD YOU BRAKE IS BASED ON HOW MUCH YOU WANT TO AVOID HITTING AN ANIMAL, NOT HOW MUCH YOU LIKE THAT ANIMAL.

YOU ONLY BEGAN TO PANIC WHEN YOU REALIZED
THAT LARGE BLACK CLOUD IN THE DISTANCE
WASN'T A TORNADO!

YOU HAVE A MUDJACKER ON SPEED DIAL.

YOU HAVE NEEDED A BLOOD TRANSFUSION AFTER A FISHING TRIP.

WHEN YOUR WIFE IS ABOUT TO COME HOME AFTER A WEEKEND AWAY, AND YOU HAVE BEEN LOAFING THE WHOLE TIME, YOU KNOW HOW TO GET THE LAWN CUT IN A HURRY!

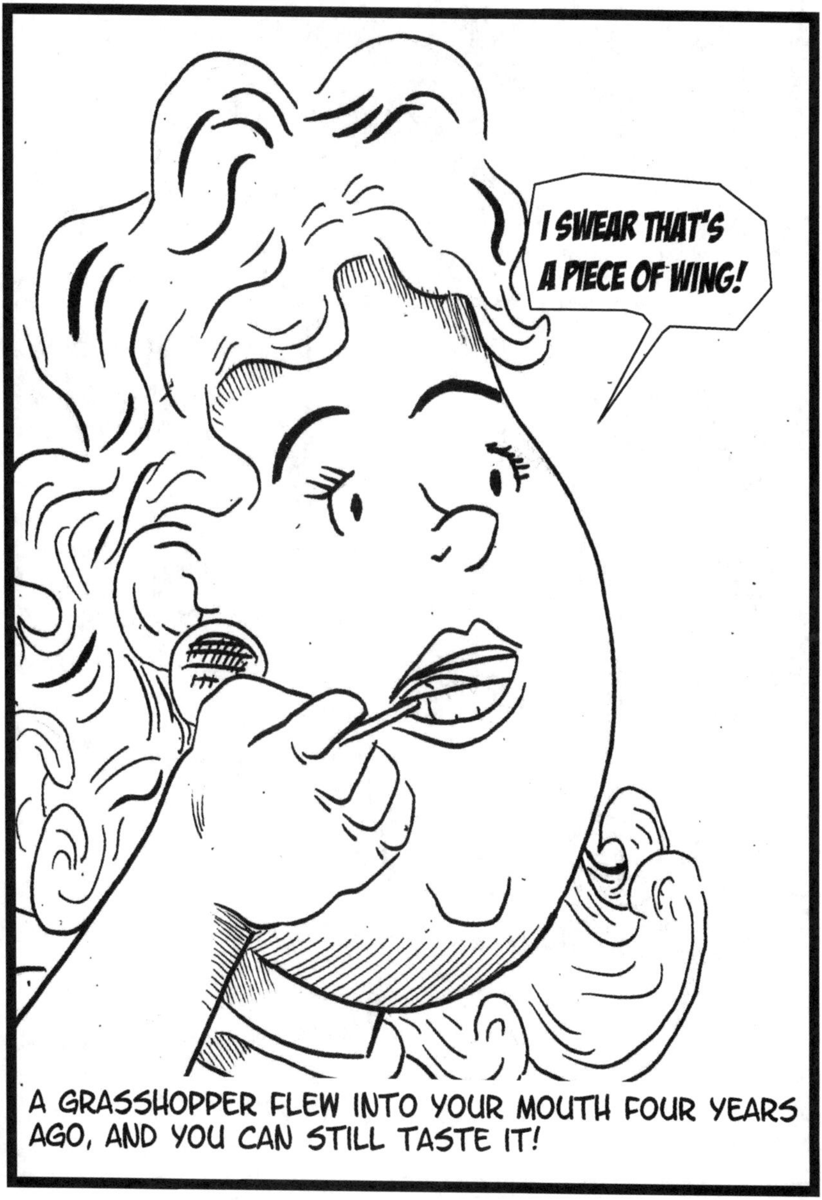
I SWEAR THAT'S A PIECE OF WING!
A GRASSHOPPER FLEW INTO YOUR MOUTH FOUR YEARS AGO, AND YOU CAN STILL TASTE IT!

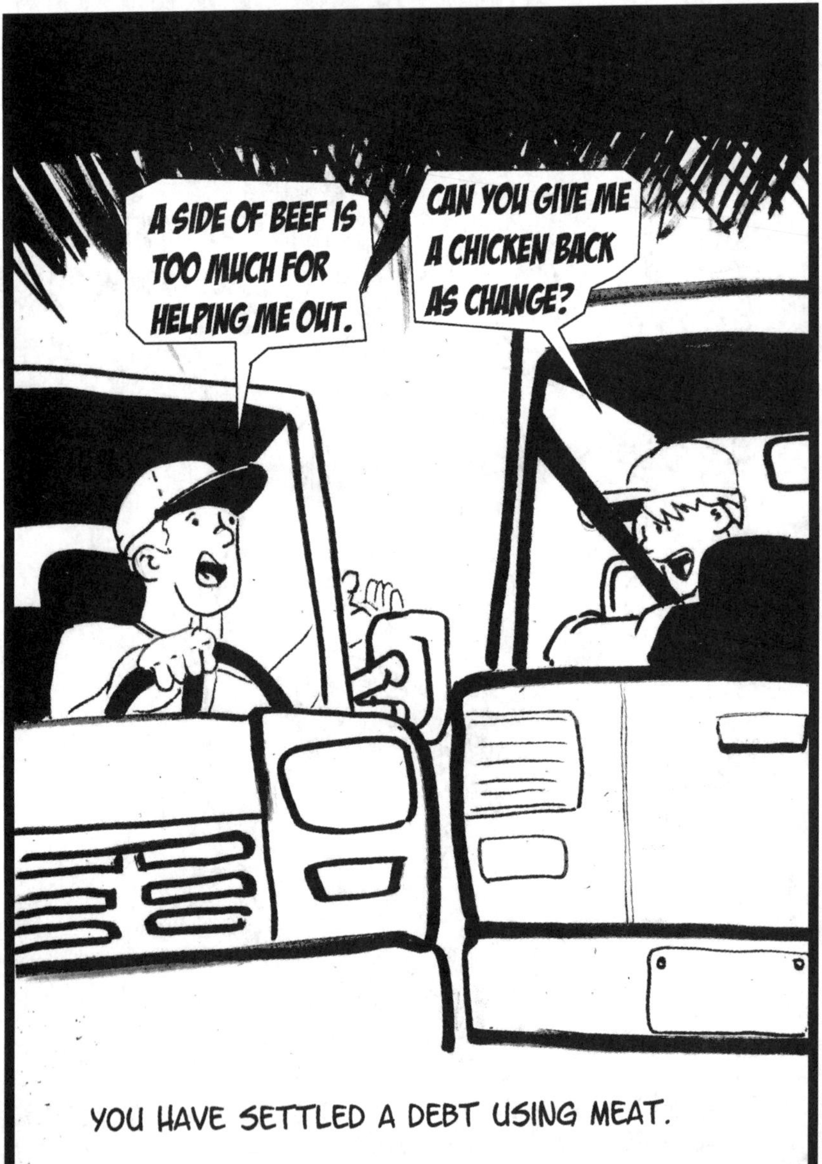
A SIDE OF BEEF IS TOO MUCH FOR HELPING ME OUT.
CAN YOU GIVE ME A CHICKEN BACK AS CHANGE?
YOU HAVE SETTLED A DEBT USING MEAT.

YOU HATE IT WHEN COWS WANDER ONTO YOUR LOCAL GOLF COURSE.

YOU LIVE IN THE LARGEST CITY IN YOUR PROVINCE, AND YOU FIND NOTHING UNUSUAL ABOUT HAVING A BARN IN THE MIDDLE OF IT.

YOU HAVE BOUGHT CLOTHING AT A STORE THAT SELLS ANIMAL FEED.

YOU OWN HORSESHOES, BUT NOT A HORSE!

YOU SECRETLY MEASURE EVERYTHING IN INCHES, POUNDS AND MILES.

YOU HAVE EATEN MORE THAN 20 DIFFERENT TYPES OF MEAT.

YOU HAVE NO IDEA WHY PEOPLE WOULD PAY MONEY TO HAVE AN INDOOR SWIMMING POOL, WHEN YOU HAVE TO PAY MONEY EVERY SPRING NOT TO HAVE ONE.

YOU'D RATHER FREEZE TO EAT FRESH FISH, THAN EAT FROZEN FISH.

YOUR KID'S SNOW FORT LASTS SO LONG THAT THE CITY INCREASES YOUR PROPERTY TAXES FOR HAVING A PERMAMENT IMPROVEMENT TO YOUR LOT.

YOUR MAILMAN REFUSES TO ENTER YOUR YARD
UNTIL SPRING.

YOU FIND WAYS AROUND YOUR CITY'S BYLAW AGAINST HAVING A CLOTHESLINE.

YOUR NEIGHBOUR WANTS TO RAISE CHICKENS, AND IT MAKES THE NEWS.

YOU HAVE GOTTEN INTO AN ARGUMENT OVER HOW MOOSE JAW GOT ITS NAME.

YOU LOOK FORWARD TO BUYING FRUIT FROM EXOTIC LOCATIONS LIKE B.C.

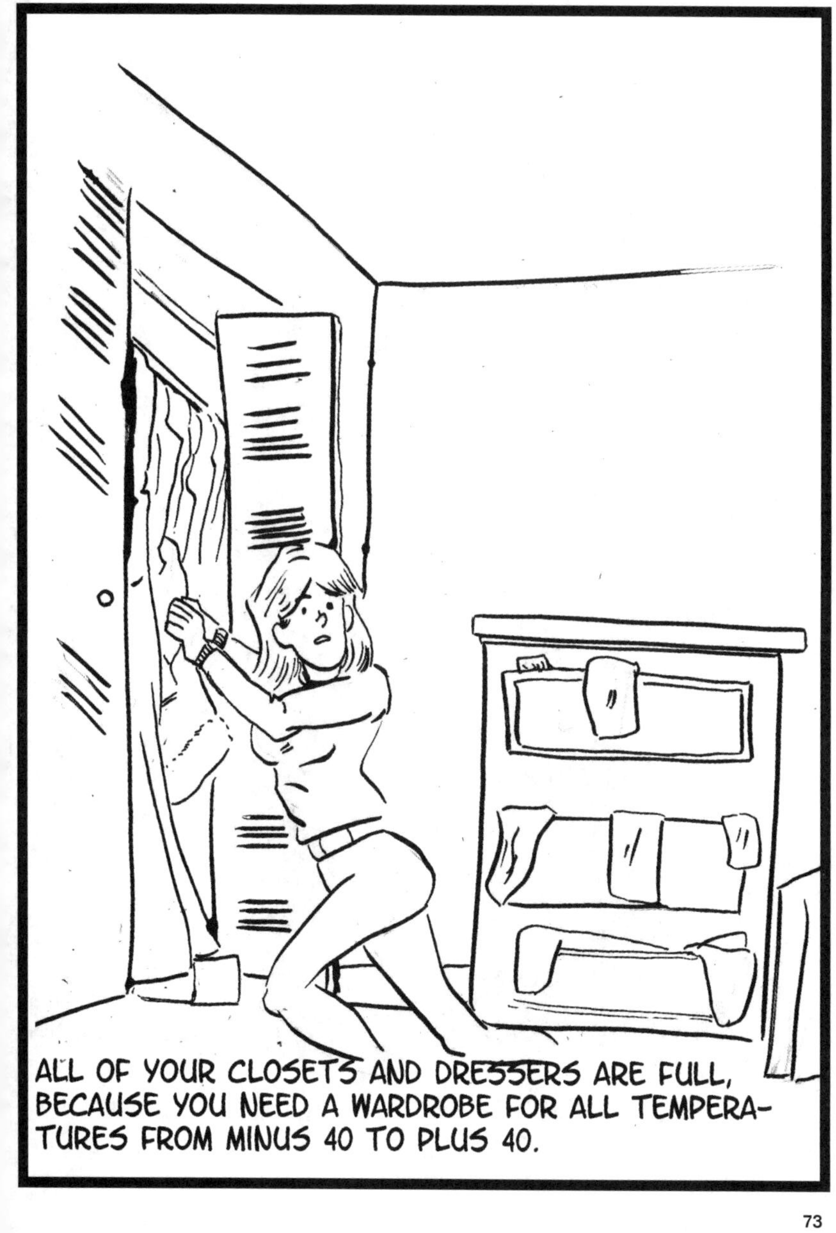
ALL OF YOUR CLOSETS AND DRESSERS ARE FULL, BECAUSE YOU NEED A WARDROBE FOR ALL TEMPERATURES FROM MINUS 40 TO PLUS 40.

THE WEATHER FORECAST CALLS FOR SMOKE.

YOU HAVE DRUNK A DOUBLE, WHILE WATCHING A DOUBLE.

YOU HAVE PARALLEL PARKED A SNOWMOBILE.

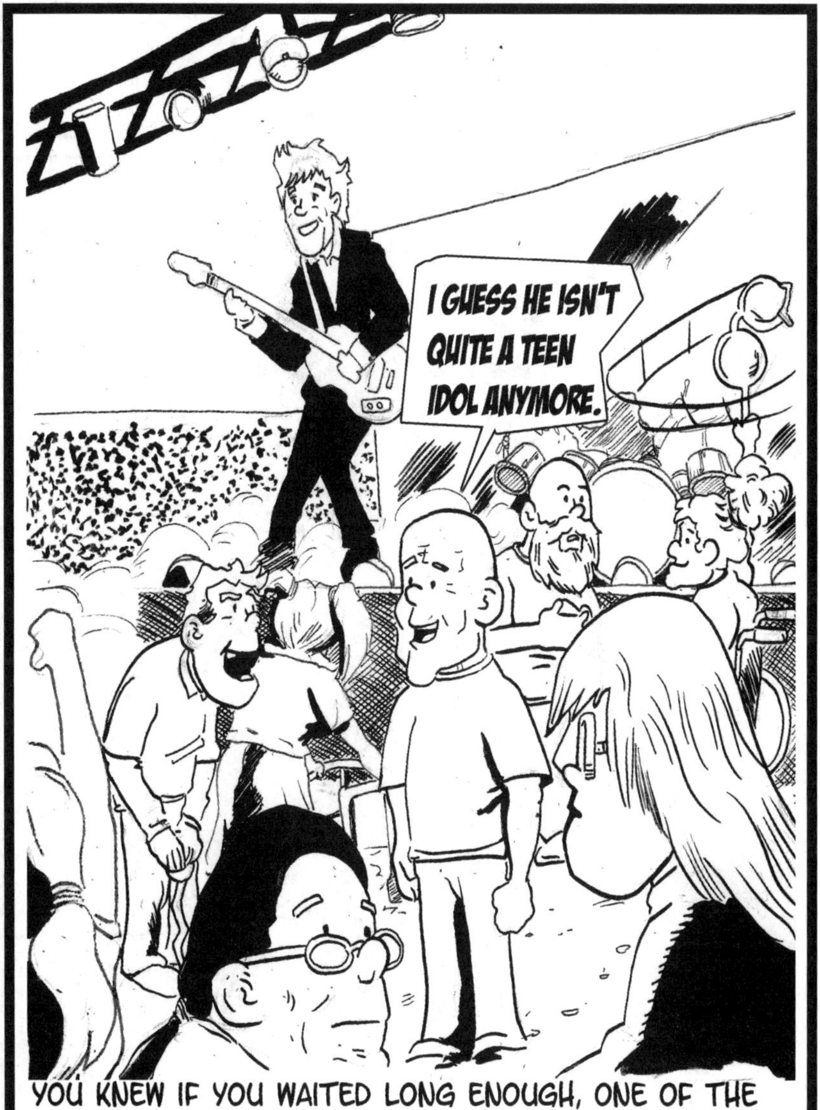
I GUESS HE ISN'T QUITE A TEEN IDOL ANYMORE.
YOU KNEW IF YOU WAITED LONG ENOUGH, ONE OF THE BEATLES WOULD PLAY REGINA.

YOUR DOG HAS MORE PIERCINGS THAN YOU.

YOUR HUNTING BLIND IS WHERE THE ACTION IS.

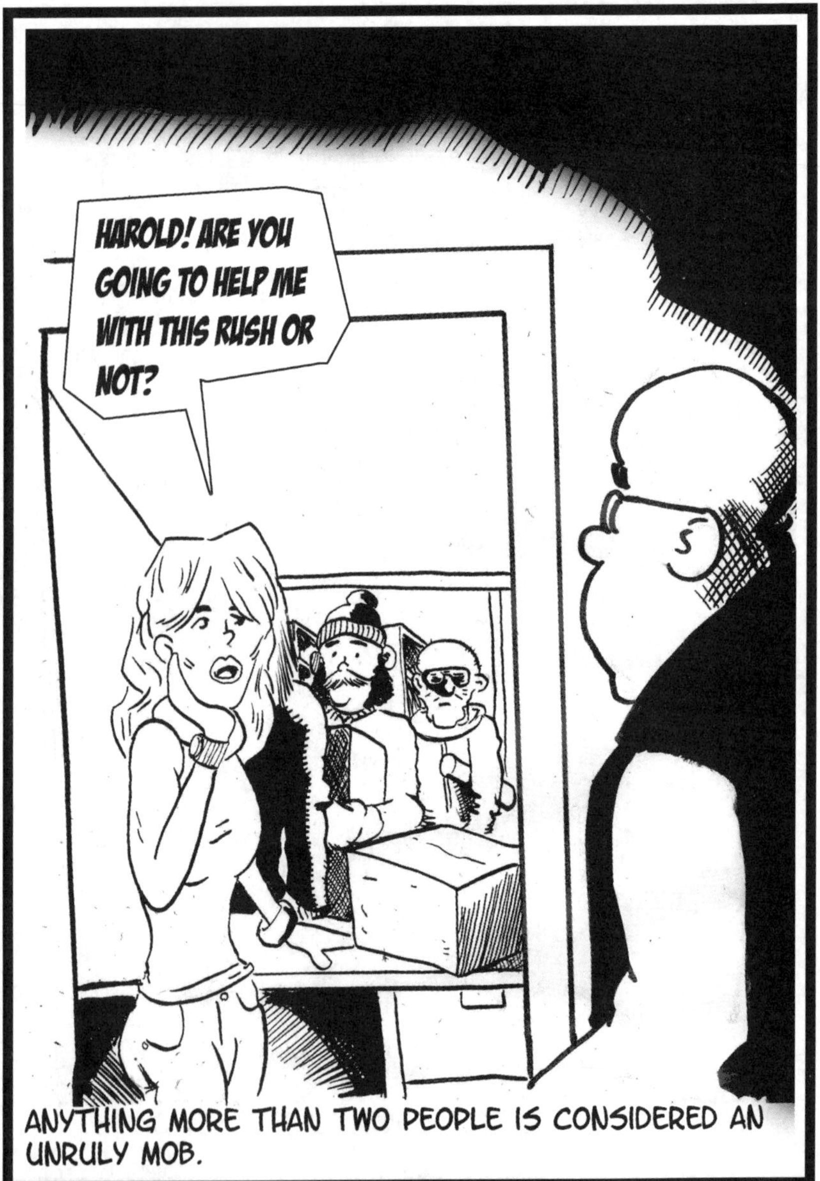
HAROLD! ARE YOU GOING TO HELP ME WITH THIS RUSH OR NOT?
ANYTHING MORE THAN TWO PEOPLE IS CONSIDERED AN UNRULY MOB.

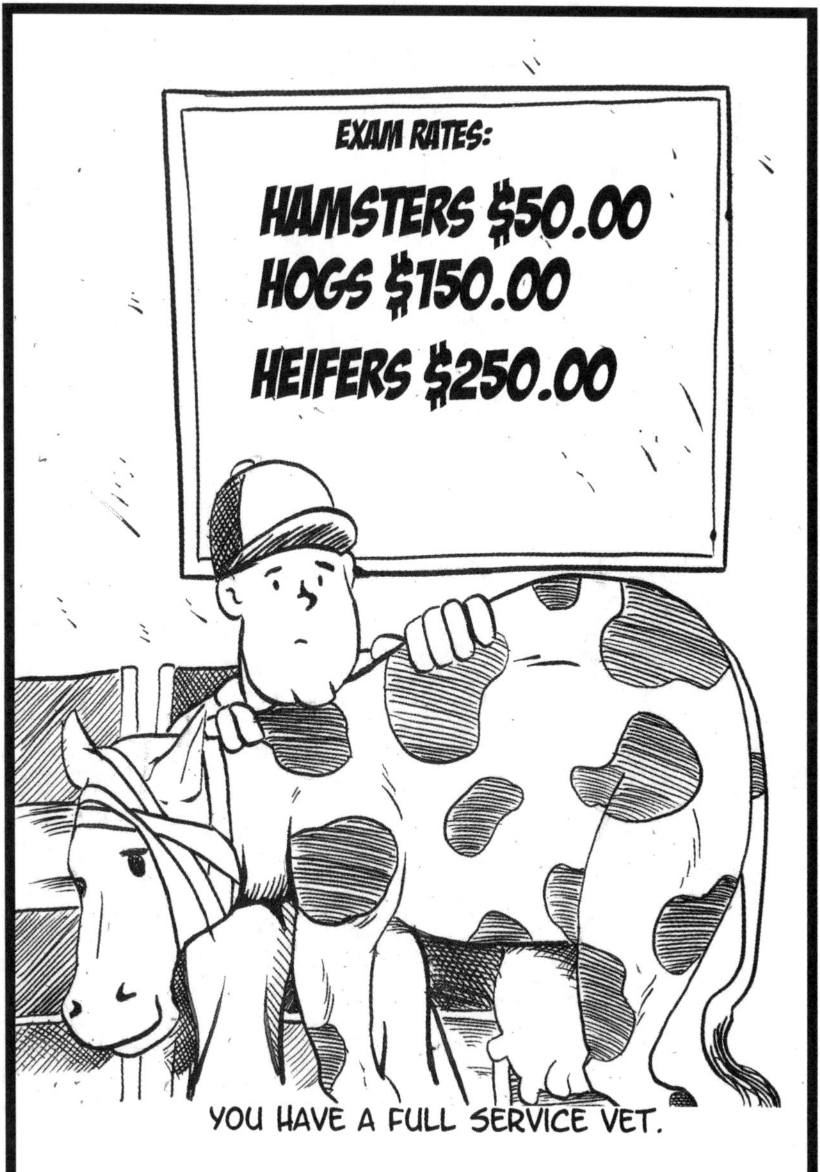
EXAM RATES:
HAMSTERS $50.00
HOGS $150.00
HEIFERS $250.00
YOU HAVE A FULL SERVICE VET.

YOUR HIGH SCHOOL GYM CLASS TAUGHT THE POLKA.

YOU HAVE HAD A " PUTTNAM'S PRAIRIE EMPORIUM" FLASHBACK.

YOU HAVE HAD A CAR ACCIDENT WITH A DEER.

INSTEAD OF GOING TO THE LAKE,
THE LAKE COMES TO YOU.

AT LEAST TWO MEMBERS OF YOUR FAMILY HAVE BEEN ATTACKED BY TWO DIFFERENT WILD ANIMALS.

YOU PUT YOUR CHRISTMAS LIGHTS UP IN AUGUST, AND
TAKE THEM DOWN IN MAY BECAUSE YOU HATE GOING ON
YOUR ROOF WHEN THERE IS SNOW ON IT.

YOUR GARAGE SALE INCLUDES HEAVY MACHINERY.

YOU OWN AT LEAST ONE ITEM BOUGHT AT AN
AUCTION BY WAVING AT A FRIEND.

YOU HAVE SEEN A GREEN AND WHITE BIRD'S NEST.

YOU KNOW THE NUMBERS OF FOOTBALL PLAYERS WHO RETIRED MORE THAN 30 YEARS AGO.

YOU ENJOY ETHNIC FOOD, BUT PREFER CANADIAN FOOD LIKE HOLOPCHI AND PEROGIES.

YOU CAN'T SEE THE END OF YOUR BACK YARD.

ONE INCH OF RAIN EQUALS A FLOOD.

YOU FOUND OUT THE HARD WAY HOW ITCHY CANARY SEED IS.

THE ONLY TRAVELLING ART EXHIBIT THAT COMES TO TOWN IS ON RAILS!

YOUR FAVORITE FISHING SPOT IS ONE MILE FROM SHORE, AND YOU CAN STILL WALK TO IT.

Before:

After:

YOUR ENTIRE FAMILY GETS SUMMER HAIRCUTS.

YOU END UP WITH THE FLOWERS YOUR NEIGHBOUR PLANTED ON A WINDY DAY.

YOU OWN A FOUR WHEEL DRIVE, AND YOU STILL GOT STUCK TWICE, IN YOUR OWN DRIVEWAY.

YOU GAVE A KID $5 TO SHOVEL YOUR DRIVEWAY, AND AFTER HALF AN HOUR HE GAVE YOU YOUR MONEY BACK AND WALKED AWAY.

YOU HAVE SEEN AT LEAST FOUR VERSIONS OF "STREET HEART" PLAY LIVE.

YOU ARE OPPOSED TO HIGH TECH, EXCEPT WHEN IT ALLOWS YOU TO WATCH THE "STANLEY CUP" PLAYOFFS WHILE FARMING.

YOU HAVE TAKEN A FAMILY OUTING TO A SNOW DUMP IN JULY.

YOU WOULD RATHER SWAT MOSQUITOES THAN SWAT KIDS HIGH ON DEET.

YOU HAVE BEEN STOPPED BY A PATROLMAN BECAUSE HE WAS LONELY.

YOU HAVE GOTTEN INTO AN ARGUMENT OVER THE CORRECT NAME FOR A WEED.

YOU OWN AT LEAST ONE BELT BUCKLE THAT IS BIGGER THAN YOUR BELT.

YOU OWN THREE SPECIES OF HAT RACK.

YOU HAVE HAD EVERYTHING IN YOUR BIRD FEEDER, EXCEPT BIRDS!

YOU HAVE SALUTED A PRAIRIE LILY.

YOU HAVE GONE TOBOGGANING DOWN A DITCH, BECAUSE IT WAS THE BIGGEST SLOPE AROUND.

YOUR IDEA OF HIGH CULTURE IS A MUD DRAG.

YOUR ALL-TIME FAVORITE SUMMER WAS WHEN YOU WENT TO A MUSTARD FESTIVAL, AND A RHUBARB FESTIVAL.

YOUR FAVORITE CONCERT HALL IS ONE WHERE YOU HAVE TO BRING YOUR OWN CHAIRS.

YOU DRESS FASHIONABLY, FROM THE KNEES UP.

YOU USE A WEATHER FORECASTING METHOD OTHER THAN THE WEATHER CHANNEL.

YOU HAVE TAKEN TIME OFF WORK FOR A HOCKEY DRAFT.

YOU HAVE GOTTEN AN AUTOGRAPH FROM A HUNTER.

YOU HAVE LEFT A PARTY BECAUSE SOMEONE WAS WEARING THE SAME BALL CAP AS YOU.

YOUR CANADA DAY FIREWORKS IS A BUG ZAPPER.

YOU QUESTION THE COMPLETENESS OF YOUR CELL PHONE'S COVERAGE.

YOUR CHRISTMAS CARD FEATURES YOU POSING
WITH LIVESTOCK.

YOU HAVE STOOD IN LINE OVERNIGHT TO BUY INSECT REPELLENT.

YOU DON'T WEAR FASHION ACCESSORIES, BUT YOUR TRUCK DOES!

AS LONG AS I PUT OUT A FRESH SALT LICK EVERY FEW DAYS THEY STAY OUT OF MY GARDEN.

YOU HAVE HAD A PEACE TREATY WITH A WILD ANIMAL.

YOU HAVE MISTAKEN PICTURES OF THE ICE AGE FOR CHRISTMAS.

YOU DRIVE EVERYWHERE IN SUMMER AND WINTER, BECAUSE YOU ARE MORE WORRIED ABOUT YOUR PERSONAL TEMPERATURE NOW THAN GLOBAL WARMING IN THE FUTURE.

YOU HAVE GOTTEN INTO AN ARGUMENT OVER THE MERITS OF VELCRO STRAP BALL CAPS VERSUS PEG AND HOLE ONES.

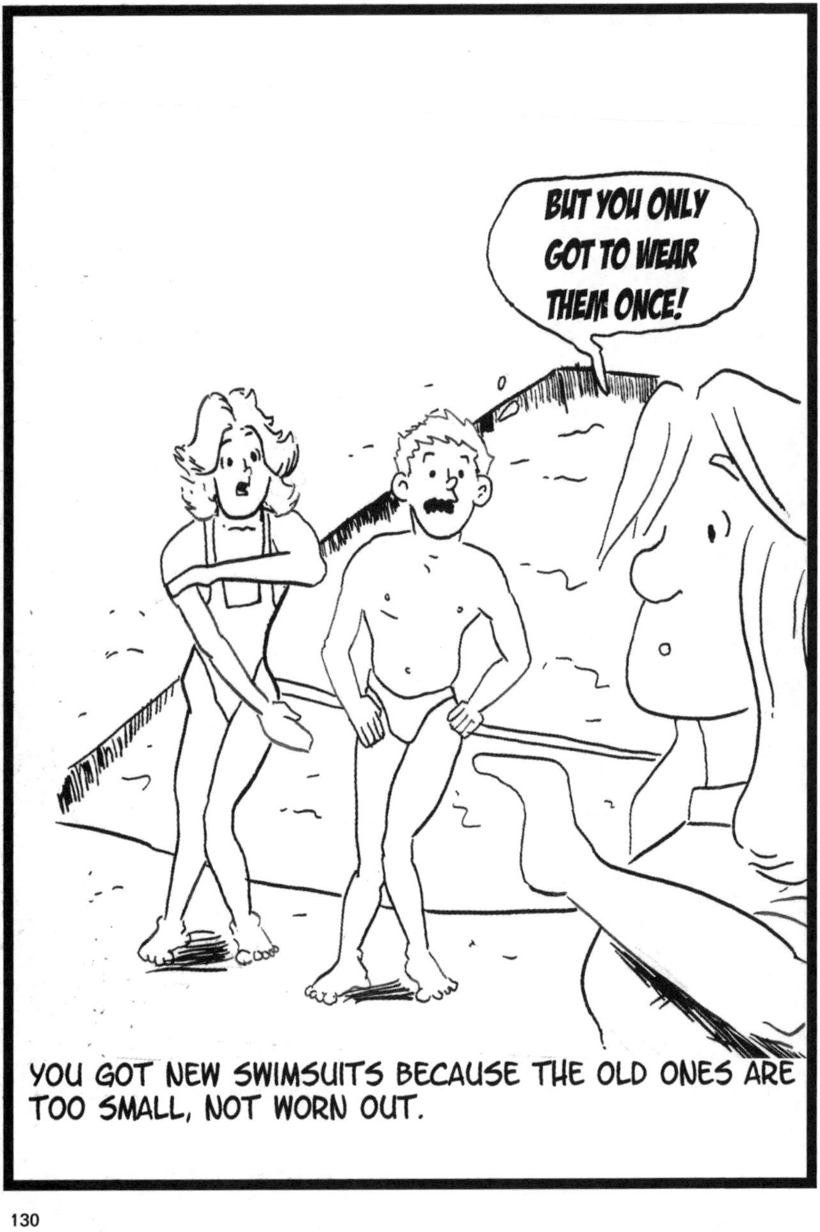
BUT YOU ONLY GOT TO WEAR THEM ONCE!

YOU GOT NEW SWIMSUITS BECAUSE THE OLD ONES ARE TOO SMALL, NOT WORN OUT.

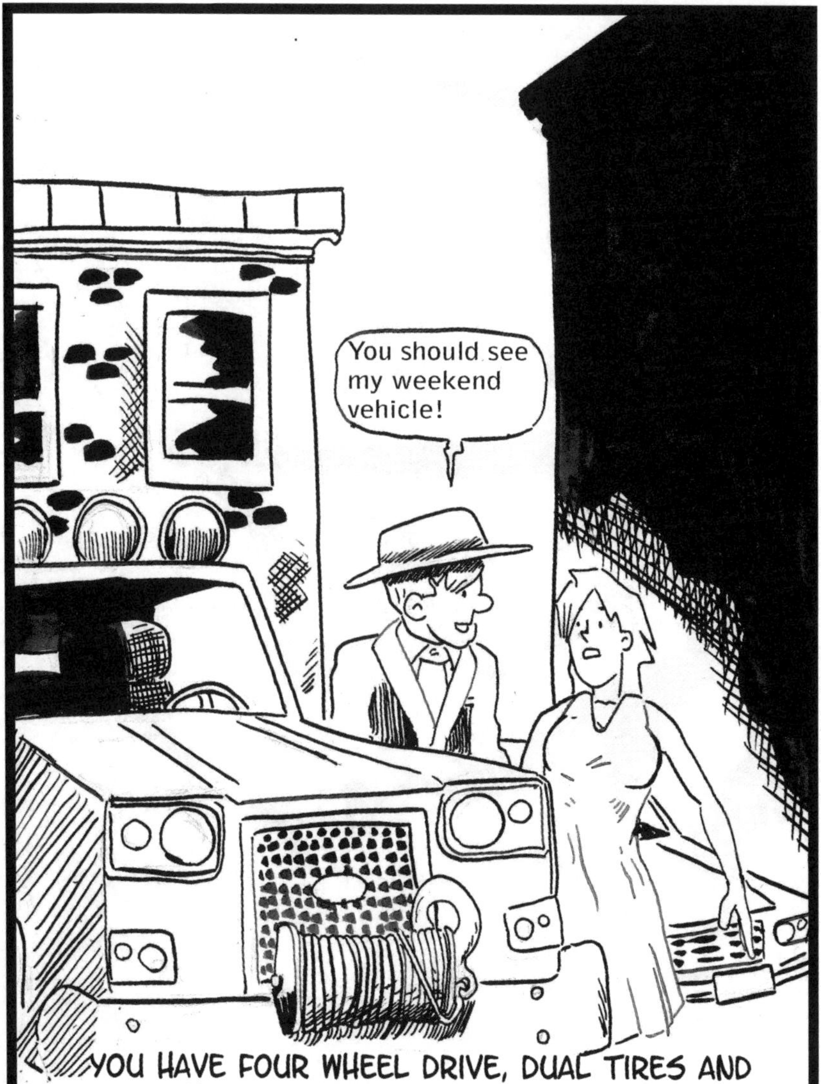
You should see my weekend vehicle!
YOU HAVE FOUR WHEEL DRIVE, DUAL TIRES AND A WINCH, AND THAT'S ON YOUR CITY VEHICLE!

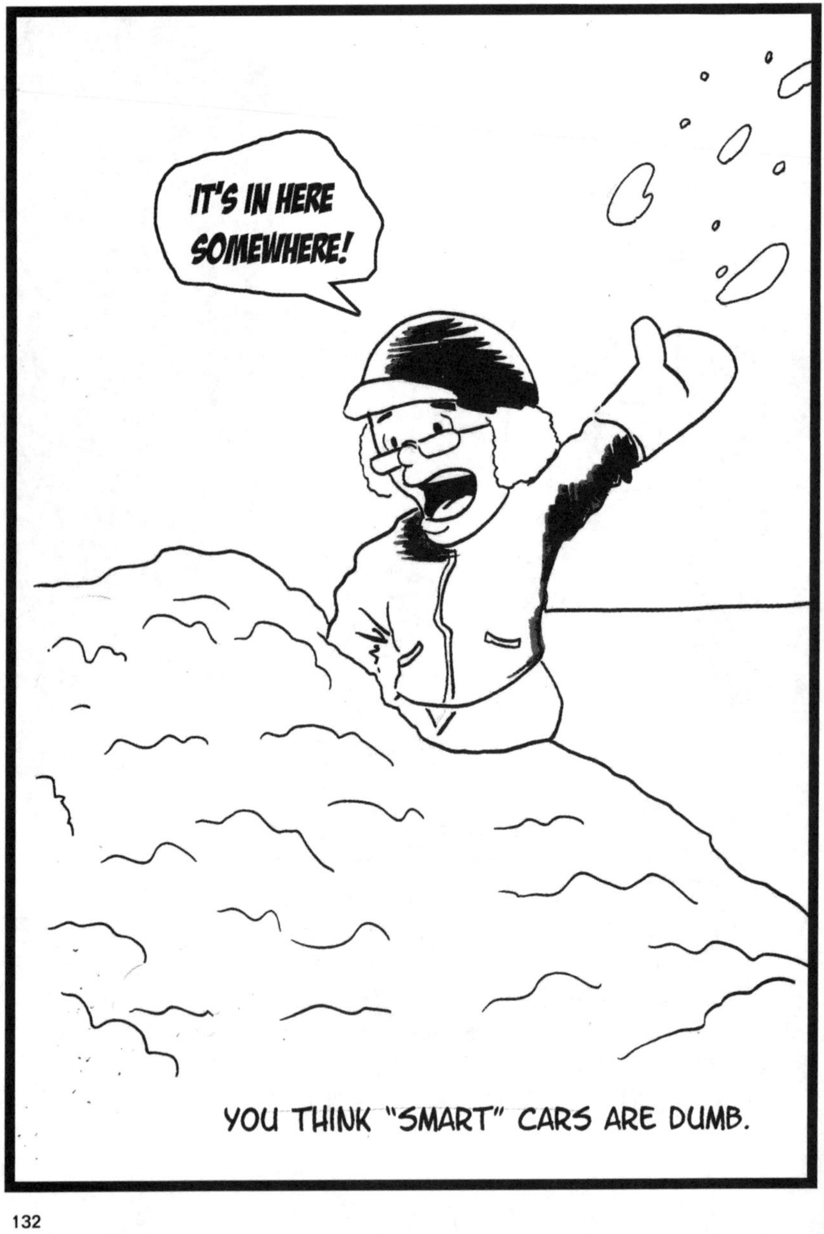
IT'S IN HERE SOMEWHERE!

YOU THINK "SMART" CARS ARE DUMB.

YOUR VACATION CONSISTS OF WORKING 10 HOUR DAYS.

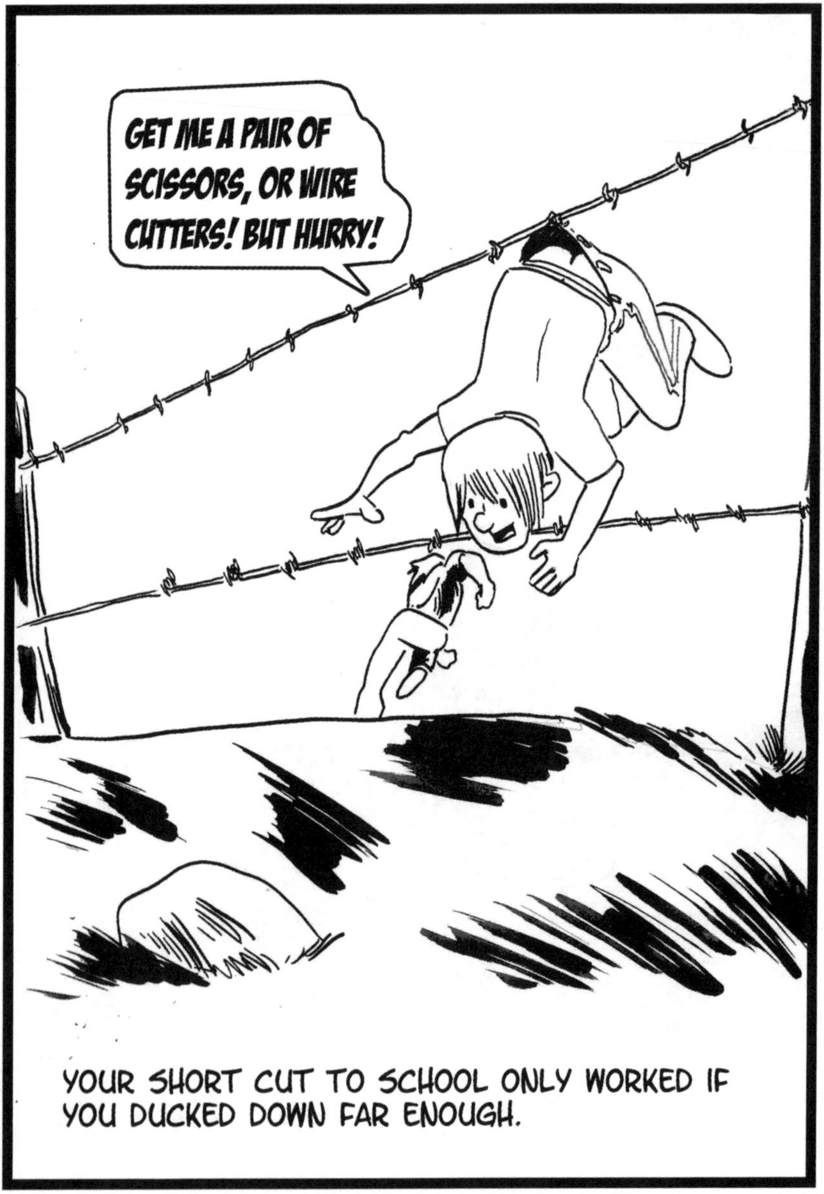
GET ME A PAIR OF SCISSORS, OR WIRE CUTTERS! BUT HURRY!
YOUR SHORT CUT TO SCHOOL ONLY WORKED IF YOU DUCKED DOWN FAR ENOUGH.

IT ISN'T GANGS OF PEOPLE YOU ARE AFRAID OF
ENCOUNTERING IN THE PARK AT NIGHT.

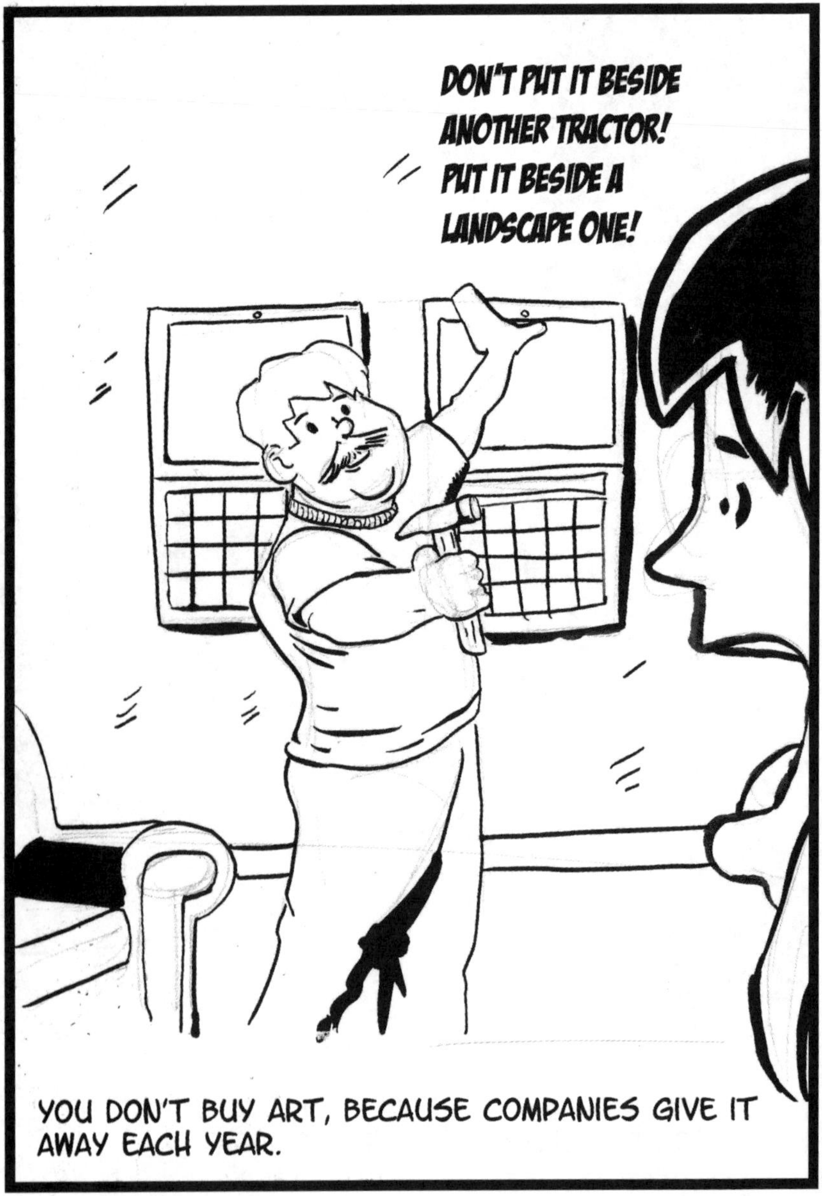
DON'T PUT IT BESIDE ANOTHER TRACTOR! PUT IT BESIDE A LANDSCAPE ONE!
YOU DON'T BUY ART, BECAUSE COMPANIES GIVE IT AWAY EACH YEAR.

YOU HAVE PUSHED A TOW TRUCK OUT OF A SNOW BANK.

YOU KNOW WHAT A PARKING BRAKE IS, YOU'VE JUST NEVER HAD TO USE ONE.

BOTH GOD AND YOUR DOG ARE YOUR CO PILOTS.

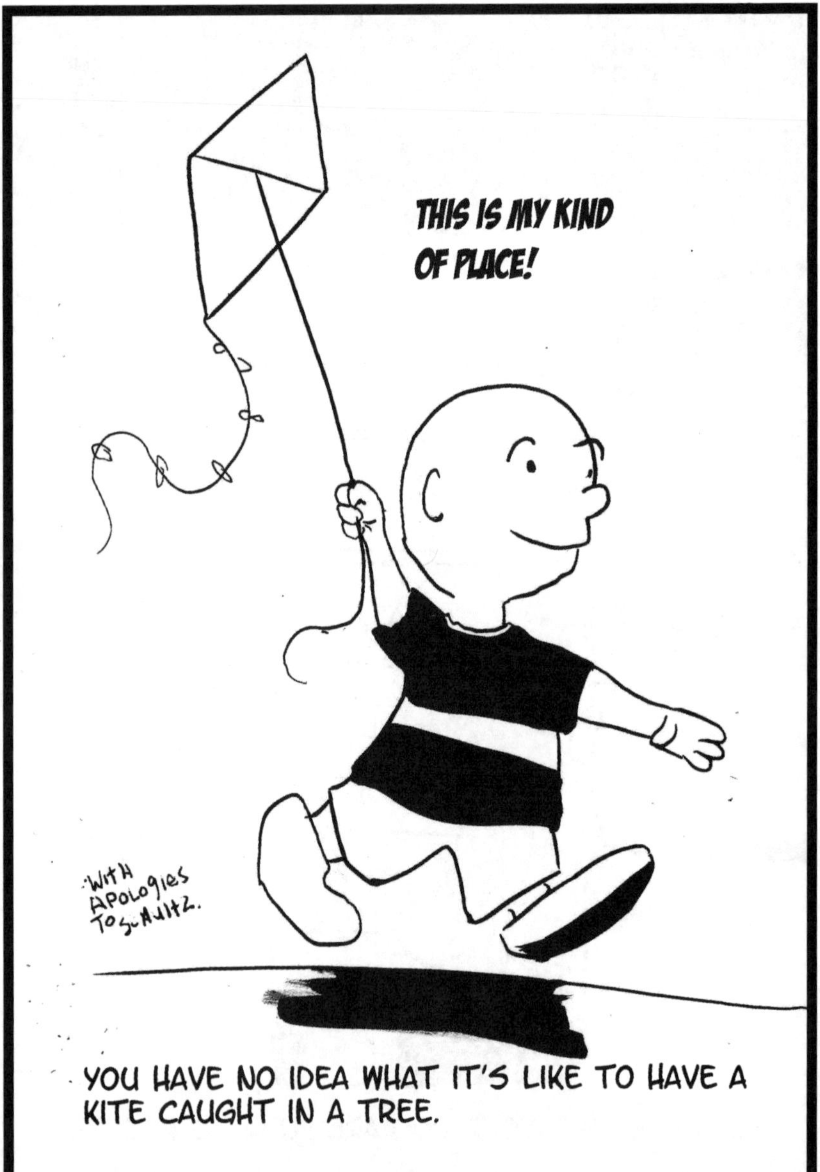
THIS IS MY KIND
OF PLACE!
WITH
APOLOGIES
TO SCHULTZ.
YOU HAVE NO IDEA WHAT IT'S LIKE TO HAVE A
KITE CAUGHT IN A TREE.

THERE ARE NO RETIREMENT PARTIES IN YOUR DISTRICT, ONLY FUNERALS.

YOU'VE NEVER HAD TROUBLE GETTING A KITE UP IN THE AIR, BUT GETTING IT DOWN CAN BE TRICKY.

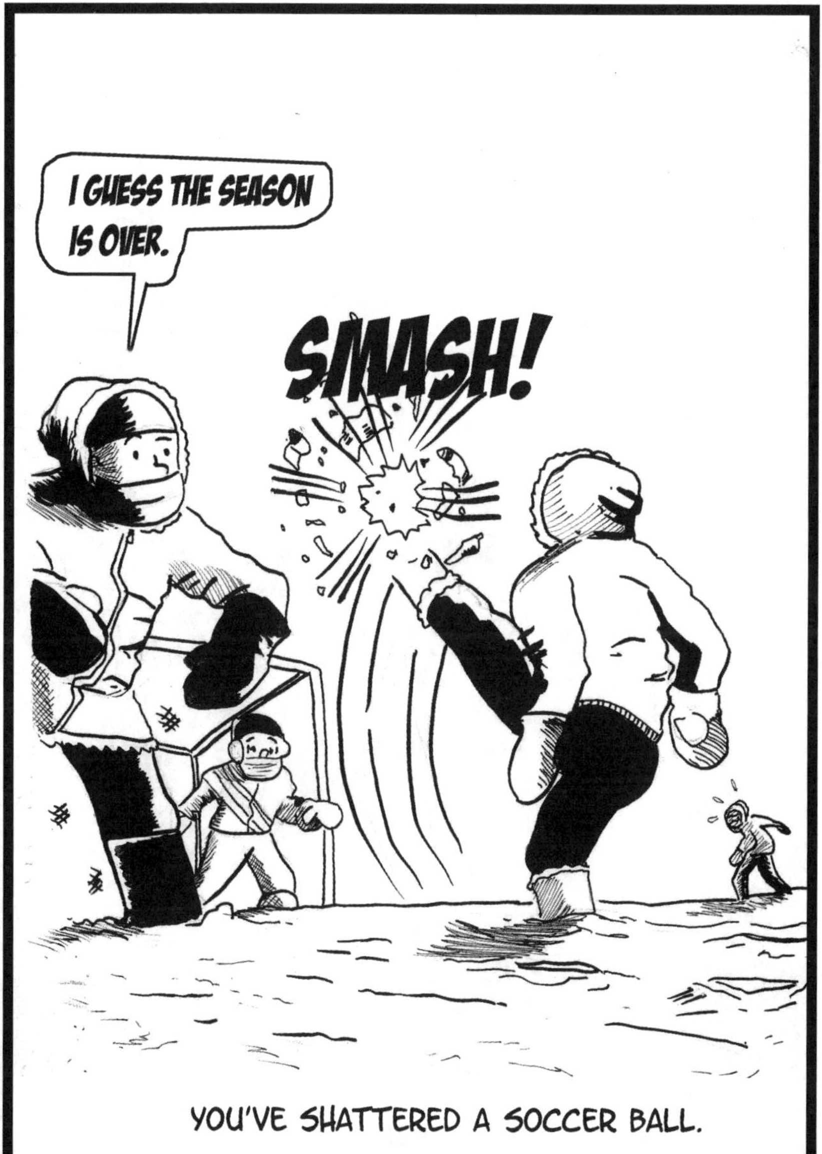
I GUESS THE SEASON IS OVER.
SMASH!
YOU'VE SHATTERED A SOCCER BALL.

YOU CELEBRATE THE ANNIVERSARY OF THE LAST WINDLESS DAY YOU CAN REMEMBER.

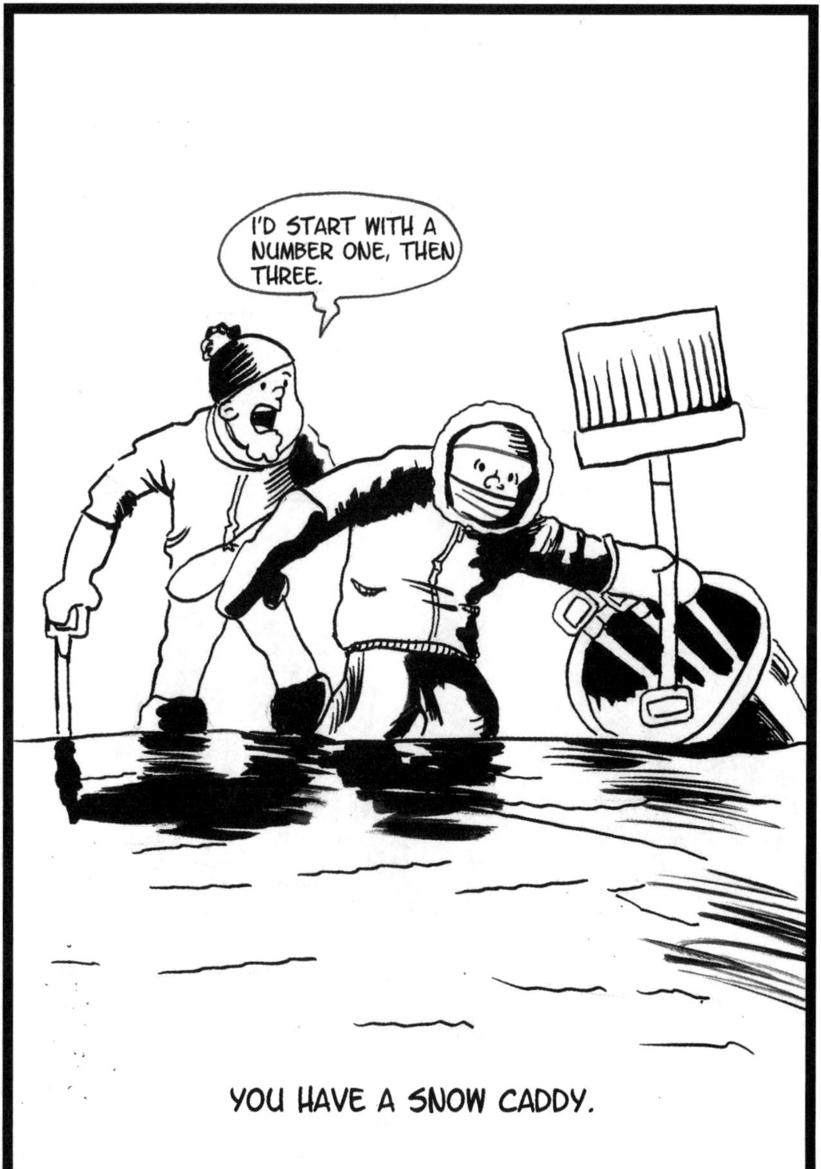
I'D START WITH A NUMBER ONE, THEN THREE.
YOU HAVE A SNOW CADDY.

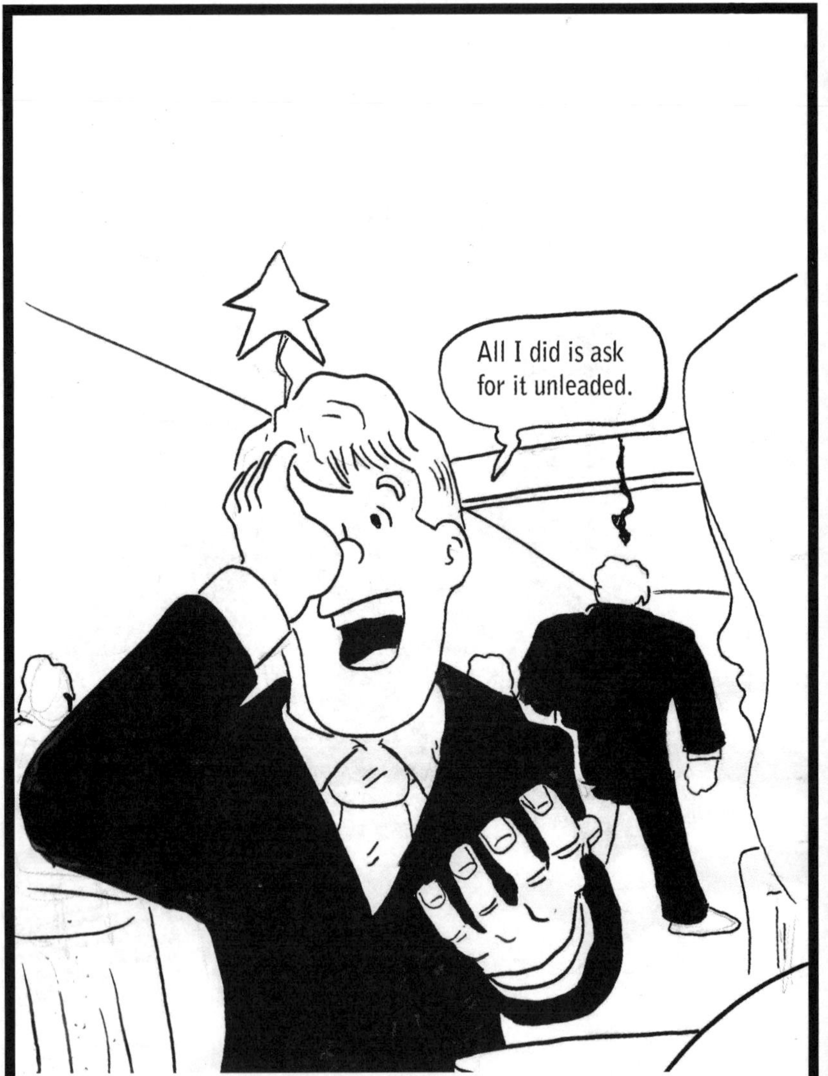
All I did is ask for it unleaded.

YOU ARE TIRED OF BULLET SOUP JOKES.

YOU AREN'T A RED NECK! BECAUSE MUCH MORE THAN YOUR NECK IS RED!

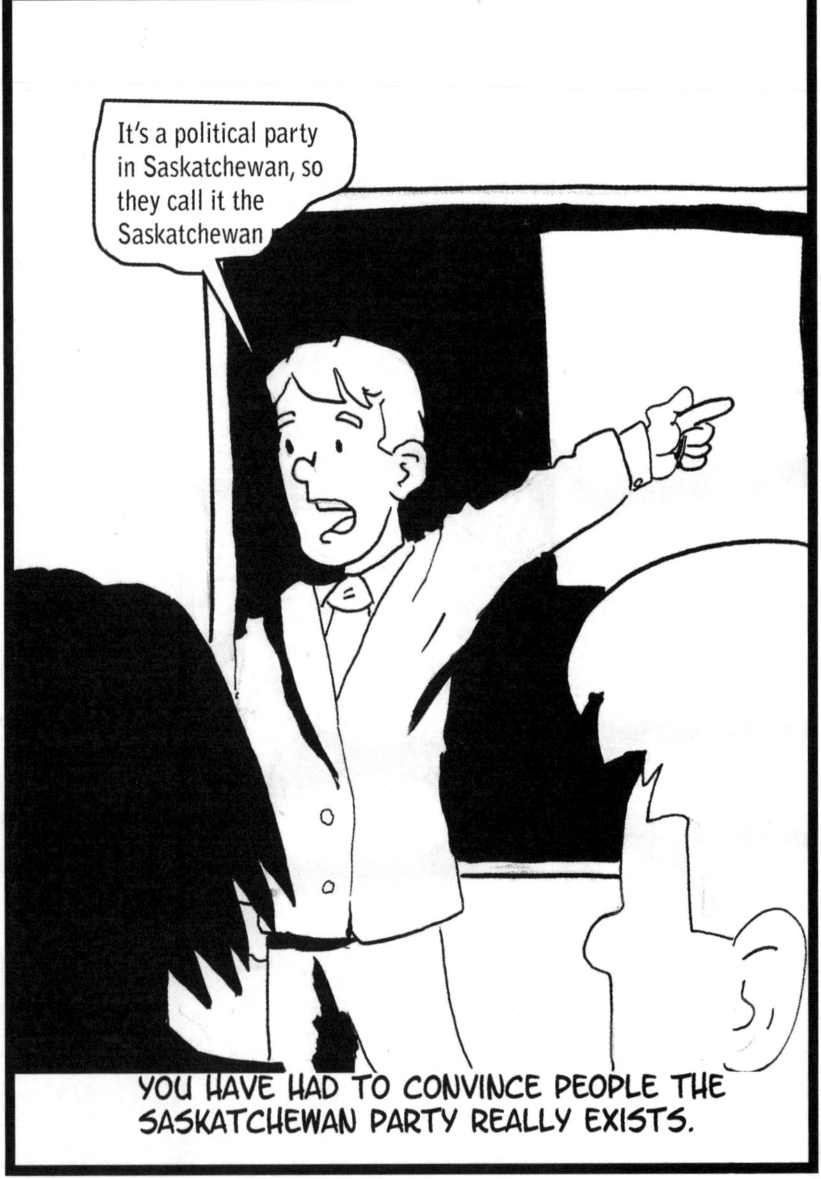
It's a political party in Saskatchewan, so they call it the Saskatchewan
YOU HAVE HAD TO CONVINCE PEOPLE THE SASKATCHEWAN PARTY REALLY EXISTS.

THERE IS NOTHING YOU WOULD CHANGE ABOUT THIS GREAT PROVINCE, OTHER THAN THE HEAT, THE COLD, THE MOSQUITOES, THE WIND AND THE ROUGHRIDERS' RECORD AT HOME.

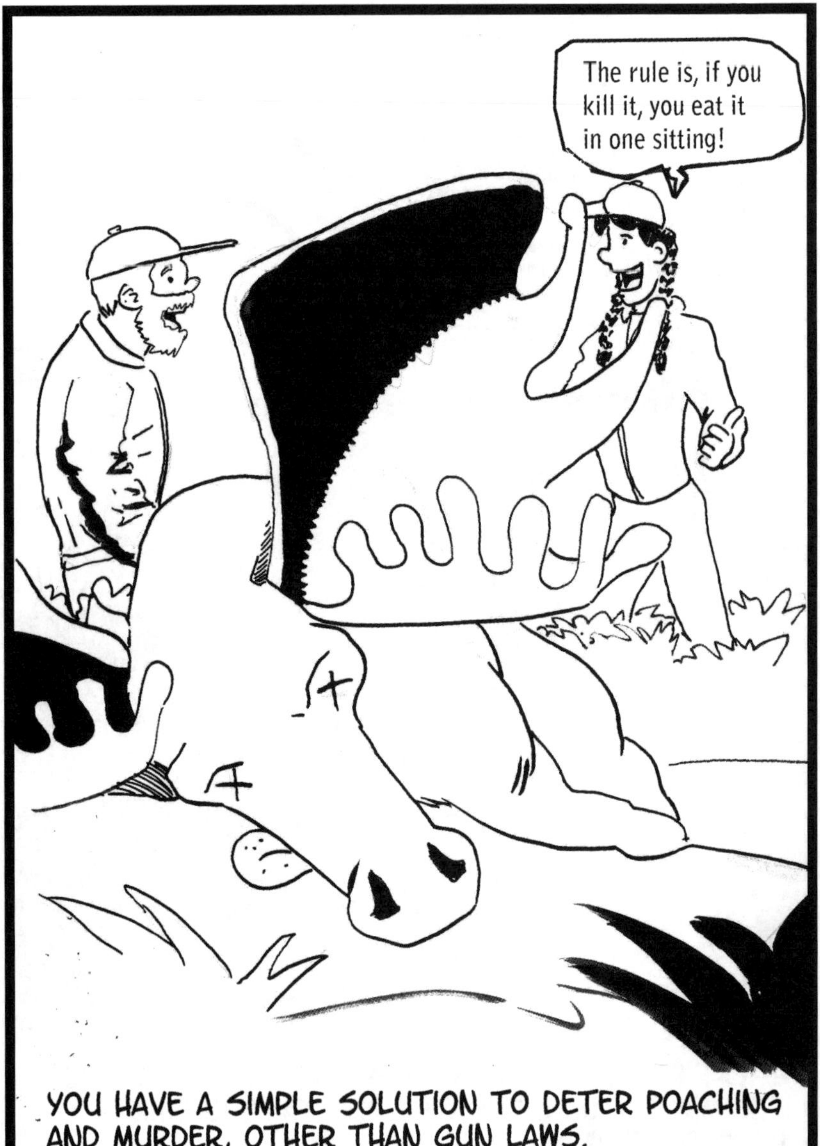
The rule is, if you kill it, you eat it in one sitting!
YOU HAVE A SIMPLE SOLUTION TO DETER POACHING AND MURDER, OTHER THAN GUN LAWS.

YOU LEFT THE PROVINCE FOR A HIGHER SALARY ELSEWHWERE, AND SPEND ANY INCREASE IN YOUR PAY ON TRAVELLING HOME EVERY CHANCE YOU GET.

YOU HAVE EXAGGERATED WHAT LIFE IN THE PROVINCE IS LIKE TO DISCOURAGE UNWELCOME VISITORS, KNOWING THEY WILL BELIEVE EVERY WORD.

YOU LOVE SASKATCHEWAN EVEN THOUGH YOU KNOW THE PAGES OF THIS BOOK AREN'T FILLED WITH JOKES; THEY ARE ALL TRUE STORIES.